Wilhelm Lilljeborg

On the Lysianassa Magellanica H. Milne Edwards

and on the Crustacea of the suborder Amphipoda and subfamily

Lysianassina found on the coast of Sweden and Norway

Wilhelm Lilljeborg

On the Lysianassa Magellanica H. Milne Edwards
and on the Crustacea of the suborder Amphipoda and subfamily Lysianassina found on the coast of Sweden and Norway

ISBN/EAN: 9783337343521

Printed in Europe, USA, Canada, Australia, Japan

Cover: Foto ©Andreas Hilbeck / pixelio.de

More available books at **www.hansebooks.com**

ON THE

LYSIANASSA MAGELLANICA H. Milne Edwards,

AND

ON THE CRUSTACEA OF THE SUBORDER

AMPHIPODA

AND SUBFAMILY

LYSIANASSINA

FOUND AN THE COAST OF SWEDEN AND NORWAY.

BY

WILLIAM LILLJEBORG.

PROFESSOR OF ZOOLOGY.

WITH 5 PLATES.

UPSALA

THE ROY. ACAD. PRESS.

MDCCCLXV.

The *Lysianassa magellanica* is one of the most remarkable Amphipods on account of its unusual size. In this respect indeed it surpasses all other animals of the same suborder, and is sometimes cited as an example of the size to which this suborder of Crustacea can attain. These in fact seldom reach the length of 1 inch, whereas the *Lysianassa magellanica* is more than 3 inches long and is moreover of stout form and strongly built. We know of a species of the family *Hyperidæ*, the *Cystosoma Neptuni* GUÉRIN-MÉNEVILLE, from the Indian Ocean, the individuals of which are more than 3 inches long, but their form is much slighter; and a species of the family *Oxycephalidæ, Rhabdosoma armatum* WHITE, found between Amboina & Van Diemens land, which attains a length of $4\frac{1}{2}$ inches, but the form of the body is almost threadlike. The *Lysianassa magellanica* may therefore be justly considered as the largest of all yet known Amphipoda.

Another circumstance renders it still more remarkable and that is its extensive geographical distribution. It has been briefly described by H. MILNE EDWARDS [1], who says, that it was found by D'ORBIGNY in the belly of a fish near Cape Horn, and was by that naturalist presented to the Museum of the Jardin des Plantes at Paris. It was accordingly a matter of considerable surprise when last autumn Mr TH. M. FRIES [2], Junior Professor of Botany, brought hither from the Norwegian Finmarken and presented to the Zoological Museum of this University three specimens of that rare Amphipod, with certain testimony, that he had received them from a shipper in Hammerfest, who had found them in the belly of an "Haaskier-

---

[1] Annales des Sciences naturelles 3:d Series, Zoology. Tome 9. 1848 p. 398, without drawings. — C. SPENCE BATE (Catalogue of the specimens of Amphipodous Crustacea in the Collection of the British Museum, 1862, p. 66. Tab. X. fig. 5) has since described and figured it after a drawing communicated by M. LUCAS. But neither the description nor the drawing is good, and the author cited seems not to have been aware of MILNE EDWARDS' previous description.

[2] We desire hereby in the name of our Science to express our thankfulness to Mr. TH. FRIES both for this and for several other similar valuable presents.

ding" *(Scymnus borealis* (Scoresby) Nilsson, on the banks by Beeren Island. The discovery of so highly developed an animal common to both the Arctic and Antarctic Oceans, was something so uncommon that it caused us to doubt the acuracy of MILNE EDWARDS' statement as regards the locality, Cape Horn, and to suspect that the specimen described by that author might perhaps have been obtained in the French Scientific Expedition to Spitzbergen, under P. GAIMARD 1838—1840. In order fully to ascertain this we have in a letter to Prof. H. MILNE EDWARDS communicated the fact that the *Lysianassa mogellanica* has been found in the neighbourhood of Spitzbergen, and we appended a drawing of the same to compare with the specimen in the Paris Museum, and asked whether the alleged locality, Cape Horn, were perfectly reliable. Mr. MILNE EDWARDS replied through his Son Mr. ALPHONSE MILNE EDWARDS that our drawing was on comparison found to correspond exactly with the specimen referred to, ("ce me parait être bien la même espèce et je n'ai pu y trouver aucune différence appréciable") moreover that it was certainly true, that that specimen had been brought by D'ORBIGNY from the Strait of Magellan, and is entered in his special catalogue of his natural-historical collections from that region.

This animal is then widely distributed both in the Arctic and Antarctic Oceans, and as it has only been met with in the stomachs of fishes it seems probable that it is only to be found at a considerable depth. Its tolerably large size and rapid motion render it difficult to catch with the so-called dredge ("bottenskrapa" Swed.), and it has not, as we have been kindly informed by Professor S. LOVÉN, been met with in the Swedish scientific expeditions to Spitzbergen.

Its being found in both the Polar seas, and not in the intermediate waters, — which however is not a unique phoenomenon — is without doubt a matter of deep scientific interest. It shows either that the same species may have several centres of origination and geographical distribution, or else that there have been periods in the developement of the earth, when certain species of animals & vegetables were, in consequence of uniform temperature and similar climatical relations, spread over the whole earth, which, on a subsequent variation of these circumstances, have retired to tracts and regions where the original and to them appropriate climate & temperature continued to prevail. It is thus that the appearance of the *Lagopus alpina* NILSSON on the fells of Lappland, on the Alps & on the Pyrenees, but not in the interjacent lowlands has been explained. There has been a glacial-period which has connected the faunas of these now widely separated tracts.

Between the faunas and floras of the Arctic and Antarctic regions, it is generally known that there prevails, a certain correspondence, so that one not unfrequently meets in both with representatives of the same family & genus, but it is extremely rare to find in both representatives of the same species, and the instances hitherto recorded appear most generally the result of confounding different species. As regards animalia vertebrata we with certainty know of only one species [1]) common to both zones, and among land-animals not one common distinguishing genus occurs. Among these the genera which are represented in both zones are in general of a cosmopolitical nature. It is among the inhabitants of the seas that we find examples of an agreement between the zones. Within the class of Mammalia such an example occurs among the Phocidae in the genus *Cystophora* NILSSON, although that genus includes a species from the West-Indian seas. From the Arctic Ocean we have the species *Cystophora cristata* (Erxl.) and from the Antarctic *Cystophora leonina* (Lin.) or *proboscidea* (Desm.) Nils., which however has by J. E. GRAY, though apparently without sufficient reason, been considered a separate genus, *Morunga*. Within the same class we have among the Cetacea the genus *Delphinapterus* or *Beluga* with two species: *D. leucas* (PALLAS) from the Arctic and *D. Kingii* (J. E. GRAY) from the Antarctic Ocean.

The feathered vertebrata or birds which on their swift wings move to distant tracts with great rapidity, not unfrequently afford, as might be expected, examples of a very extensive geographical dispersion, and we find in the Arctic zone many species common to Europe, Asia and North America, which have been termed circumpolars, and others that are extended from the polar circles to the Equatorial regions. Nevertheless perhaps not

---

[1]) *Otus brachyotus* has been mentioned by D'ORBIGNY as found at the Strait of Magellan, but GOULD considers it to be a different species and calls it *Otus Galapagoensis* as also occurring in the neighbourhood of the Galapagos Isles (Voyage of Beagle), but SCHLEGEL has since (Museum des Pays-Bas) quoted that form, marking it however with a note of interrogation, under the name of *Otus brachyotus.* D'ORBIGNY has also taken up the *Procellaria glacialis* as found in the Strait of Magellan, but it has since been found to be of a distinct species, and has even been referred to another genus, *Thalassoica* REICHENBACH, *Thalass. glacialoides* Reich. *Bonap.* D'ORBIGNY has further stated that *Hirundo rustica, urbica* and *riparia* as well as *Totanus fuscus* are found in Patagonia, but in this also he appears to have confounded different species.

more than one species can be named, that is common both to the Arctic and Antarctic zones. This is the *Falco peregrinus* Lath., which has indeed received several different specific names, as the slight varieties of colour which it displays in widely separated localities, have by some ornithologists been looked upon as indicating different species, though for our own part we cannot but agree with SCHLEGEL [1]) in considering these as merely local varieties. The variety that occurs in North & South America has been called *Falco anatum* BONAP., and the Australian form has been named *Falco melanogenys* GOULD.

The fishes found in the fresh waters of Patagonia consist, it appears, only of two or three species of the Salmonoid family, as is also the case with the fresh water fish belonging to the most northern fauna.

Among the section of Mollusca are some instances which present the phœnomenon of an extensive geographical distribution, though their capabilities for locomotion are very limited. Thus for example the *Terebratula caput serpentis* is found from Spitzbergen to the Mediterranean and on the eastern coast of North America, and the *Rhynchonella Psittacea* from Spitzbergen and Greenland to England, Massachussets and Sitcha on the western coast of N. America. Some species e. g. *Saxicava arctica*, *Venus pullastra* and *Pecten pusio* are found both on our northern coasts and at the Cape of Good Hope though not in the intermediate tropical regions. We may perhaps be able to show with certainty any species distinctly belonging to the Arctic Zone, which also occurs in the Antarctic, though one or two peculiar genera have been found that have their representatives in both Zones. BRONN [2]) states that the species of *Limacina* which belongs to the south Polar Ocean can not be distinguished from the *Limacina arctica* belonging to the northern, but it has by WOODWARD [3]) been classed as a separate species with the name *Limacina antarctica*. That genus has no representatives in the intermediate seas. The same is the case with the genus of *Puncturella*, which embraces two species, of which the one belongs to the arctic the other to the antarctic seas (in the neighbourhood of Tierra del Fuego). Of the genus *Clio* we have in the northern Polar Seas the *Clio borealis*, which is there found in such plenty as to constitute a considerable portion of the Greenland WHALE's food. Passing over the intermediate oceans

---

[1]) Museum des Pay-Bas. 1 Livraison. Falcones. p. 1.

[2]) Klassen und Ordnungen des Thierreichs. 3. Bd. p. 648.

[3]) Manual of the Mollusca p. 207.

that genus is according to WOODWARD represented in the Antarctic Ocean by some few species, but according to H. & A. ADAMS[1]) by only one, the *Clio australis* BRUG. The genus of *Buccinum*, including about 20 typical species, also belongs only to the arctic and antarctic seas. The same is the case with the genus *Trophon*, containing about 14 species, the chief part of which are from the Northern Seas (WOODWARD).

The Bryozoa often present examples of more widely spread geographical distribution than other animals of the lower section, and of these the same species have been occasionally met with in both the arctic and antarctic seas. Thus for example the *Retepora cellulosa*, which is not uncommon in our arctic region, has by Ross been found at a depth of 1620 feet in the South Polar-Sea[2]), *Lepralia Malusi* BUSK, at Cape Horn, in the Mediterranean and in northern Europe, and *Flustra foliacea* ESPER in the Southern Ocean and in Northern Europe[3]).

The difference between the Crustacea, which strictly belong to the Arctic & Antarctic Zones, is not so great as that between them and those which are found in the warmer seas, but we know as yet of only 2 species common to both, both of the lowest group, and only a few peculiars genera common to both Zones. Our knowledge af the Crustacea of the Antarctic Regions is however as yet so imperfect as not at present to justify the uttering of a decided opinion on the relation, that may exist between the antarctic & the arctic Zones in this matter. The following genera are common to both zones. Order *Podophthalmia*: *Lithodes* LATR., *Munida* LEACH, *Euphausia* DANA[4]). Suborder *Amphipoda*: *Orchestia* LEACH, *Anonyx* KRÖYER, *Iphimedia* H. RATHKE, *Atylus* LEACH, *Amphithoë* LEACH, *Hyperia* LATREILLE, *Themisto* GUÉRIN-MÉNEVILLE, *Cyamus* LAMARCK. Suborder *Isopoda*: *Idothea* FABRIC., *Glyptonotus* EIGHTS, *Porcellio* LATR., *Oniscus* LIN., *Jaera* LEACH, *Sphaeroma* LATR.[5]); Order *Copepoda*: *Cetochilus* ROUS-

---

[1]) The genera of recent Mollusca. T. 1. pag. 62.

[2]) Bronn: Klassen und Ordnungen etc. 3 Bd. p. 90.

[3]) Ibid. p. 92.

[4]) Mr TH. FRIES has kindly presented to our University's Zoological Museum some specimens of a Schizopod that appears to constitute a link uniting the *Euphausia* DANA with the *Thysanopoda* M. EDWARDS, found by him after a storm thrown upon the shore of Warangerfjord in the norwegian Finnmarken. The last pair but one of the truncal feet has only the outer branch or palp, very small, and an almost imperceptible rudiment of the inner branch or stem. We shall call it *Euphausia glacialis* n. sp., as it appears to approach somewhat nearer to the genus *Euphausia*.

[5]) We have found at Öresund (the harbour of Landskrona) a species of the

SEL DE VAUZÉME; Order *Cirrhipedia: Lepas* LIN., *Balanus* LIN., *Coro-nula* LAM., *Verruca* SCHUMACHER. Of these genera only the *Lithodes, Ano-nyx, Themisto* and *Glyptonotus* are peculiar to the Zones in question. The others are of a cosmopolitical nature, and are met with also in the temperate and torrid Zones. This is partly the case with the genera *Anonyx* and *Themisto*, but the greatest number of the species in those genera as well as, with respect to the first named genus, the greater plenteousness and larger dimensions of the individuals, sufficiently indicate preference for the polar seas and more especially the northern. The genus *Atylus* according to SPENCE BATE [1]) numbers 16 species. Of these 4 are from Greenland, Sweden and Norway, 3 from England, 2 from Southern Europe, 1 from N. America, 1 from Valparaiso, 3 from Tierra del Fuego, 1 from the Cape of Good Hope and one from New Holland. It belongs then more especially to the cold & temperate waters, but is however in a very considerable degree of a cosmopolitical nature [2]).

Of the 4 above-named distinguishing genera, *Lithodes* comprises 10 species, of which 6 are from the northern seas — North-Sea, N. Atlantic and Icy Ocean and from the NE-coast of Asia — 1 from the eastern coast of America, *Lithodes australis* BELL [3]), and 3 from Tierra del Fuego and the Antarctic Ocean; *Anonyx* about 28 species, of which 20 are from Green-land, Sweden and Norway and England, 4 from the Eastern coast of N. America, 3 from the seas of Nort-eastern Asia, and one from Tierra del Fuego; *Themisto* 5 species, of which 2 are from the Antarctic Ocean, 1 from the southern part of the Atlantic & 2 from Greenland (S. BATE); and lastly *Glyptonotus* 3 species, of which 2 are from the northern Icy Ocean and Baltic and 1 from the southern Icy Ocean. The genus *Lysianassa* M. EDWARDS, of which SPENCE BATE reckons 15 species, comes so near the genus *Anonyx* Kröyer, that we as yet have no certain characteristics, by which these two genera can be distinguished, and it is probable that KRÖYER would not have set up *Anonyx* as an separate genus, had he been aware that also the 2:d

---

genus *Sphaeroma, S. rugicauda* LEACH, which has as yet never been discovered on the western coast of Norway, but probably exists there.

Whether the species of the genus *Iphimedia* found at Tierra del Fuego belong reaally to that genus is not quite certain.

[1]) Catalogue of the specimens of Amphipodous Crustacea etc. p 133.

[2]) *Atylus carinatus* (FABR.), which had previously only been found in Green-land, we have met with at Molde and Christiansund in Norway at a depth of 40—50 fathoms.

[3]) British Stalk-Eyed Crustacea, p. 164.

pair of the truncal feets have a claw. If we unite the two genera, the geographical distribution will require some little modification, as becoming somewhat less arctic or antarctic. Of the 13 species of the genus *Lysianassa* 2 are from Greenland and Norway, 7 from the Mediterranean, the Atlantic, England and Norway, 1 from Van Diemens Land, 1 from the Cape of Good Hope, and 2 from Rio Janeiro. None of these species is common to both the arctic and antarctic seas. We have not included the *Lysianassa magellanica* in this calculation, because, as we in the following pages shall show, it constitutes the type of a separate genus. In fact the Cirripeds are the only other order, in which we have examples of species common to both these zones, for the *Lepas Hillii* and *fascicularis*, which are spread over the whole earth (DARWIN), are also found in both the above mentioned zones.

The genus *Glyptonotus* has been formed by EIGTHS [1]) to define a gigantic species of the Idotheidæ, found in South Shetland, which approaches the *Idothea entomon* and is accordingly generically united with it and with the *Idothea Sabini*. It has been called *Glyptonotus antarctica* EIGTHS (according to DANA). This genus, the geographical distribution of which is, as we have before stated, confined to the polar tracts, although the one species, *Glyptonotus entomon* (LIN.), as a relic of an extinct glacialfauna (S. LOVÉN), is still occasionally found in more southern parts, as for instance in the Baltic, accordingly presents a most striking and remarkable example of the coincidence of disposition that exists between the two marine polar faunæ. The consideration of this lessens in some degree our astonishment, at the discovery of so higly developed a species as the *Lysianassa magellanica* common to both the arctic and antarctic zones.

Professor TH. FRIES has been kind enough to furnish us with some information relative the Flora of the arctic and antarctic Zones, which we here communicate, as being a valuable assistance in judgeing of the relation between the Faunæ of these Zones. "Among the vegetable productions of antarctic America there are not a few found that also belong to the Flora of Europe. The greater part of these however consist of such easily acclimatized species as *Senecio vulgaris*, *Taraxacum officinale*, *Sonchus oleraceus*, *Galium aparine*, *Brassica campestris*, *Capsella bursa pastoris*, *Stellaria media*, *Urtica urens* etc., which are now found, one may say, spread over the whole world. Among the vegetables which cannot be referred to this

[1]) Transact. Albany Institute. II. pag. 331. (according to DANA).

class, we especially remark certain hill plants common to the mountains
of Europe and those of the antarctic Zone, but not met whith in the intermediate tracts. Of these HOOKER enumerates *Erigeron alpinus, Carex festiva,
Phleum alpinum* and *Trisetum subspicatum*, but it is probable that on closer
examination these will be found to be nearly related but different species.
A remarkable example of a species common to both the Arctic and Antarctic regions and not met with elsewhere, is afforded by the beautiful
and easily distinguised moss-species *Usnea melaxantha*, which is met with
in Greenland and Spitsbergen as well as in New-Zealand and the most
southerly portions of America. The only difference between the northern
and southern forms is that the latter seems more thriving and fructifies
richly, whereas the former is a more delicate plant and has never yet
been met with in a fructificating state. It is also curious that a so remarkably distinct form as the *Nephroma arcticum*, which is so generally met
with in the northern alpine and subalpine regions, should nowhere else be
represented by any analogous or similar form excepting at Magellan's
strait, where the very similar and nearly related *Nephroma antarcticum* is
met with. Among phanerogamous plants the genus *Empetrum* presents the
same phœnomenon, being in the North principally represented by the *E.
nigrum*, whereas in antarctic America the *E. rubrum* is the prevailing
species, unless (as I have lately seen asserted) this latter be also found
in Northern America."

We now proceed to describe the remarkable Amphipod *Lysianassa
magellanica*.

It differs in many important features very considerably from the other
species included in the subfamily *Lysianassina*, and we are accordingly in-
duced to consider it as the type of a separate genus. The first basal joint
of the lower antennae is large and swelling, and uncovered at the side
of the head, and is limited above by a projecting point of the shell of
the head, which gives the head, when seen in profil a peculiar appearance. The first pair of maxillae is furnished with a thin and long palp,
at the end of which are two or three coarse bristles or small prickles.
The 7th caudal segment or caudal appendage, which is deeply forked,
is not provided with any moveable spine at the extremity of the lobes.
At least one such spine is found in all other Lysianassina which have the
caudal appendage forked. On account of its extensive geographical distri-

bution, we give to this genus the name *Eurytenes* [1]), and characterize it in the following manner:

EURYTENES, nov. gen.

Corporis forma crassa et robusta, epimeris magnis et pedibus brevibus. Antennæ superiores flagello appendiculari prædita, pedunculo crasso et ejus segmentis 2:do et 3:tio brevibus, et flagelli segmento 1:mo longo. Antennæ inferiores segmento pedunculi 1:mo magno et inflato et extus visibili. Mandibulæ palpigeræ acie lævi et tuberculo molari magno instructae. Maxillae 1:mi paris palpo biarticulato angusto, apice duas vel tres setas vel aculeos minores mobiles gerente, et earum ramus interior latus et brevis et setis multis ciliatis instructus. Maxillipedum lamina trunci segmenti 2:di, sive lamina exterior margine interiore tenuissime noduloso, et eorum palpus quadriarticulatus et unguiferus. Pedes trunci sive thoracici 1:mi et 2:di paris subcheliformes, illi validi et breves, ungue bene evoluto, hi longiores et graciliores, ungue minutissimo. Reliqui pedes trunci forma solita, robusti. Laminae branchiales simplices minimeque pectinatim plicatae. Pedes caudales ultimi paris ramis lamellosis. Segmentum 7:mum sive ultimum caudae profunde bifidum, laciniis acuminatis ad apicem vero non spiniferis. — Tantummodo una species:

EURYTENES MAGELLANICUS (H. MILNE EDWARDS)

Lysianassa magellanica, H. MILNE EDWARDS: Annales des Sciences naturelles, 3:me série, Zoologie, Tome 9:me; 1848: pag. 398.

„   „ C. SPENCE BATE: Catalogue of the specimens of Amphipodous Crustacea in the Collection of the British Museum, pag. 66, tab. X, fig. 5. — 1862.

Description: Length of body from end of caudal feet $2^{15}/_{16}$ inches or 73 millim. The three specimens we possess, which are all females, are all of the same size. Form of body (Pl. I. Fig. 1) stout and strongly built, with the 2:nd to 4:th pairs of epimera (*coxae* S. BATE) large, with the truncal feet, with the exception of the 2:nd pair, short and strongly formed. The 1:st truncal segment's epimera less than usual with that group, which causes the base of the lower antennæ and the appendages of the mouth to appear exposed. The last segment of the trunc and the first 5 of the tail have above a low longitudinal ridge, and the 6:th tailsegment has above on both sides a ridge, extending backwards, and terminating in a compressed obtuse

---

[1]) From the Greek εὐρυτενής, which signifies widely stretched.

process. The 4th truncal segment's epimera, which are the largest, are almost rhomboidal with the corners rounded off, and with a wide hollow at the upper and back corner. The 5th pair of epimera are almost rectangular with the corners rounded off, and a little hollow in the middle of the lower edge, into which hollow the upper edge of the 5th pair of feet's second joint is inserted. The epimera of the 1st tail-segment have the lower and back corner rounded off, and those of the 2nd segment have the same corner extented into a short point, from which on the outer side of the epimera a tolerably sharp edge or ridge (Fig. 21) stretches itself obliquely upwards and forwards. The 4th tail-segment's epimera have at their lower extremity a large spine turned backwards.

The eyes are not visible and have accordingly not been introduced in the figure of the animal, but seem, judging from the inner portions, to have been large and kidney- or bottle-shaped, and red.

The head (fig. 2) is somewhat convex, the forehead almost truncated, and has in the middle only an obtuse angle, as a slight indication of a rostrum. On the sides of the head is a projecting obtuse-angled lobe between the upper and lower antennæ. The hollow under that lobe is terminated at its lower extremity by a projecting process.

The shaft of the upper-antennæ is short, and its first joint longer than the two following together, and the 2nd a little longer than the third. The flagellum consists of about 27 joints, the first of which is a little shorter than the shaft, and has on the inner side numerous long thickly set bristles of a brownish colour. The flagellum when laid back reaches about to the middle of the 2nd thoracal segment. The flagellum appendiculare or appendage, which is but litttle shorter than half the flagellum, consists of 9 joints of which the first is the longest.

The lower-antennae are more than double as long as the upper, and their flagellum consists of about 56 joints furnished with long bristles on the under-side. The first joint in their shafts (Fig. 1 & 2, b') is especially large and distended, and for the greatest part of its length unprotected by the head-shield. The 2nd segment of the said shaft has on its underside evidently a sharp process. ("Olfactory denticle," S. BATE).

The upper and underlips (Fig. 3, c & fig. 4 & 5), which are about 5 millim. long, are of a very complicated construction. The former constitutes the central piece (a) and the latter the two side pieces (b, b) which are united at the base so as to be in some degree moveable, and can approach to or recede from one another like jaws, to which they have some resemblance. The external build is composed partly of thinner chitinous laminae and partly of more solid chitinous ribs which form the solid support of the former. The upper lip is somewhat distended and convex and has near its apex a sharp indentation, from which that apex bends itself inwards almost like a bird of prey's beak. The middle portion of the inner or palate side has two bristley-ribs united both in front and back and diverging in the middle, separated at the back by a notch from the curved apex of the beak. The side-pieces of the under lip are more solid but thin and flattened though uneven. (Fig. 5. *b, b* from the exterior, fig. 5 from the interior). At the projecting, free, indented end (*a*) they are yellowish, and their inner edge from the point to the base is armed with a thick row of short bristles, so that they are evidently employed in dividing the animal's food and conveying it to the swallow. The mandibulae are inserted between the upper and lower lips and are thus for the greatest part of their length separated from the maxillae.

The mandibulae (Fig. 3. *d. d* and figg. 6 & 7, the left) are about 5½ millim. long and peculiarly strongly formed. The masticating extremity (Fig. 6 *a* from the interior) which is bent inwards as we see it in fig. 7. *a*, has a sharp, cutting and even or toothless edge. This edge has but a slight groove on each side, from which proceeds on the inside a curved and somewhat raised line. At the middle of that line is a very small and simple accessory process ("processus accessorius", BRUZELIUS[1]), and from that a raised edge thickly armed with at first somewhat coarser and longer but afterwards shorter and finer bristles, which afterwards passes over to the "tuberculum molare" BRUZELIUS, (*b*) of which it forms the outer edge, and when there is thickly set with short bristles. Between these outer edges the tuberculum molare is hollowed out. On the fore side of the mandibula about halfway between the masticating end or edge and the insertion of the palp is a strong almost ball-like notch (Fig. 6. *c*). The palp (*d*) is large, and consists as usual of 3 joints of which the middle one is the largest and longest, and is broadest in the middle, and it, as well as the 3 joint, carry a number of sharp bristles. The palp reaches to about the end of the last joint but one of the lower antennae's shaft. Fig. 7 shows the left mandibula seen from the outer side. As the masticating extremity

---

[1] Bruzelius (Skand:s Amphipoda Gammaridea) denies the existence of such a process in the genus *Anonyx*; we have however found it in the most species.

is sharp and cutting, it is probable that it serves to divide the food, which is afterwards ground by the tuberculum molare [1]).

The first pair of maxillae (fig. 8) are also of a strong and solid construction, and their length about 7 millimètres. The outer branch [2]) (*a*) is, at the upper end (a'), spread out somewhat in the manner of a hand, hollowed on the inside, and armed at the edges with 11 stout moveable spines, which with the exception of some few of the longest are furnished on the one edge with side-prickles. The same branch's inner edge is also bristled. The inner branch (*b*) is thin, soft, short, and broad, and has at its point about 11 ciliated bristles. The palp (*c*) is two-jointed and reaches beyond the point of the outer branch. The second joint is in the form of a sabre and has a pair of short bristles at the point, as also a pair of very small moveable prickles. These maxillæ are in immediate contact with the mandibulae.

The 2nd pair of maxillae (fig. 9) are smaller thinner and of less solid construction. Their length is 5 millim. They consist of two branches, and are of about the same obtusangular lancet-form, and the outer (*a*) ⅓ longer than the inner (*b*). Both have at the point and along the inner edge numerous ciliated bristles.

The maxillipeds (Fig. 3 *g g* & fig. 10) are 10 millim. long, and consist as usual of a stem of 2 joints (fig. 10. *a*, *b*) and of a palp (*c*). On the inner side of the basal joint of each maxilliped is an oblong almost truncately terminated lamina (lamina interior) which at the point and the inner border bears a number of longer bristles. These laminae (Fig. 11) come into contact with eachother, and form by their union a raised ridge on the inner side of the maxillipeds, and reach to the end of the first third of the second joint's lamina. The second joint of the stem (Fig. 10 *b*) is on the inner fore-part expanded into a large almost elliptic lamina, the so called *lamina exterior* (fig. 3. *g'. g'* & fig. 10. *b'*), rounded off in front and there furnished with bristles. Its Interior edge (fig. 12), is made uneven by small knobs. The Palp (fig. 3. *g'' g'* and fig. 10. *c, c*) consists of 4 joints of which the 2nd is the largest, and the fourth has the form of a claw, and all, with the exception of the last, are furnished with numerous bristles.

_____

[1]) Spence Bate considers that this form of the mandibule indicates that the animal consumes vegetable food.

[2]) The outer branch may be considered as the stem of these maxillae.

The truncal feet[1]) of the first pair (fig. 13) are short, particularly strongly built and subcheliform. Their length is about 15 millim. The 2ⁿᵈ joint[2]) is the longest and the hand or 6ᵗʰ is almost rectangular, rather smaller at the lower end, with the fore edge somewhat bent and the back concave and bearing about 9 clusters of bristles. Its lower end is obliquely hollowed out, and in front of the notch is fastened a strong, sharp, crooked and flexible claw. The 5ᵗʰ joint which is triangular is shorter than the 6ᵗʰ. Its feet are without gill-sack and lamina to cover the eggs.

The truncal feet of the 2ⁿᵈ pair (fig. 14), which are also subcheliform, are finer and longer than the preceeding. Their length is about 30 millim., and the breadth of their 2ⁿᵈ joint is 2 millim. The 3ʳᵈ joint is scarcely half so long as the 2ⁿᵈ, which is almost of uniform breadth and somewhat bent back at the lower end. The hand or 6ᵗʰ joint is shorter than the 5ᵗʰ, oblong and of almost uniform breadth, and obliquely rounded off at the lower end. It has numerous long bristles, as have also the joints already described. The claw is very small and hardly perceptible. The lamina for covering the eggs (b) and the gill-sack (c) are fastened to the 1ˢᵗ joint or epimerum (a). The former is narrow and of uniform breadth, and bordered with long bristles; the latter simple, of considerable size, and almost kidney-shaped. One observes on it only a few small irregular wrinkles which have probably arisen after death.

The 3ʳᵈ and 4ᵗʰ pairs of truncal-feet (fig. 15, right foot of 3ʳᵈ pair) are similar to each other and about 24 millim. long. The 4ᵗʰ joint is longer than the 5ᵗʰ, terminated obliquely at the lower end, where, at the obtuse projecting point, it is provided with long bristles. The 6ᵗʰ joint is about the same length as the 4ᵗʰ, almost uniformly broad, somewhat curved, and at the back border provided with bristles. The claw is strong.

The truncal-feet of the 5ᵗʰ—7ᵗʰ pairs (fig. 16, the 6ᵗʰ pair, right foot) bear a close resemblance to eachother, and differ from all the preceeding

---

[1]) We here adopt the denominations proposed by T. THORELL., (Öfvers. af Kongl. Vetensk. Akad:s Förh 1864. pag. 9) according to which that part of the body of the Crustacea, which is commonly called *thorax*, is denominated trunc (truncus), and that part, which by other writers is called *abdomen*, is denominated tail (cauda).

[2]) The joint which we call the 2ⁿᵈ has in general been considered as the 1ˢᵗ. We consider that that part, to which the gill-sack and lamina for covering the eggs are attached, is the first, although it may be joined to the epimerum, or perhaps more correctly speaking (according to SPENCE BATE) constitutes what is called the epimerum. The gill has no doubt an insertion similar to that of the Podophthalmia.

in having the 2nd joint strongly expanded, and in being directed forwards. The foot of the 6th pair here represented is 24 millim. long. The 5th pair, as may be seen in fig. 1, is distinguised by having the 1st joint larger, and the back part somewhat higher than the forepart, which is almost semi-circular. The second joint is shorter, and has the posterior spreading portion almost semicircular. In those of the 6th pair this joint is rounded ovally, and the border rough with indentations or notches. These inden-tations are only slightly apparent in the 5th pair. At the base of the la-mina for covering the eggs, attached to these last mentioned feet the fe-male genital aperture is very clearly apparent. The 7th pair of truncal-feet differ from both the preceeding in having the 2nd joint longer and oval, with small but clearly visible indentations in the back border.

Each pair from the 2nd to the 5th inclusive is provided with laminae for covering the eggs, all of the same form as that, which is represented in our plate, and which belong to the 2nd pair: the 6th and 7th pairs are destitute of this appendage. In the 2nd, 3rd and 4th pairs the gill-sack is of the same form (fig. 14 c). In the 5th and 6th pairs it presents the same form (fig. 17), but differs from the preceeding in being of a firmer structure, and having a caecum-like appendage (b) containing granulated matter, con-sisting of fat globuli and other formative particles. In the 7th pair this appendage is wanting, but in other respects its gill-sack is similar to that of the foregoing pair.

The tail-feet of the first 3 pair's, or so-called swimming-feet, are of the usual form (fig. 18, 1st pair, right foot) and are similar to eachother excepting that they diminish in size, so that the 3rd pair are shorter than the foregoing. They consist of a strong, oblong stem, (a) tapering towards the lower end, and two terminal branches (b, b) tapering gradually to a point, longer than the stem, composed of a great number of joints, and on both sides provided with long ciliated bristles. The 1st pair are 19 millim. long.

The tail-feet of the last 3 pairs (i. e. the 4th, 5th & 6th) are as usual formed for leaping, and consist of a stem and two simple terminal branches without swimming-bristles. The 2 first pairs are as nearly as may be similar to one another, but are longer and have their terminal branches more pointed than those of the 6th pair. Those of the 4th pair (Fig. 19, right leg. outer side) are somewhat longer and slenderer than those of the 5th; their length is about 14 millim. Along the outside of the stem there is a raised ridge, and a similar elevation runs along the middle of both terminal branches both on the outer and inner side, though higher on the former, and highest on the outer branch (a): This branch has at its point a spine, separated by a suture, and may by this be distinguished from the inner (b), which is moreover somewhat shorter and broader.

The tail-feet of the last or 6 th pair (Fig. 20, right foot) are shorter, broader and more moveable. Their length is 8 millim. The stem is almost rhomboidal, with the lower external angle projecting acutely. The external terminal branch (a) is also somewhat longer than the internal (b) and has also a detached spine at the point. Both branches have about the same shape, are tolerably thin, though thicker at the outer edge, of a broad lancet form, and are provided with numerous bristles on the inner border. Also the stem has similar bristles on its inner border and at the outer and lower acute angle. These feet stretch somewhat behind the ends of the other tail-feet and even somewhat further back than the 7 th tail-segment.

The 7 h tail-segment or, as it is called, caudal appendage (fig. 21) is of considerable size, extending almost to the ends of the last tail-feet. Its length is 6 millim. It is forked a little below the middle, and the opening between the two halfs somewhat wider towards their termination. It is tolerably thick with a blunt ridge which on both sides goes parallel with and close beside the external edges of the lobes, with a hollow along the middle between the base and the opening. The lobes are brought up smoothly to points, and are destitute of the moveable spines at the end, and no spines are visible on their sides.

The Group of the family *Gammaridae*, which the subfamily *Lysianassina* constitutes, seems to be tolerably natural and well defined, but it happens with it, as with many other natural groups, e. g. *Felidae* among mammalia, *Cyprinidae* among fishes, etc., that the forms belonging to it, especially the different species within the same genus, not unfrequently present such slight differences, that it requires a very minute examination to distinguish them. This group is distinguished by the form of the upper antennæ and mandibulæ, the former having a peculiarly thick shaft of which the two last joints are very short, and the latter a more or less sharp edge with few or no teeth (fig. 52), and the inner process (a) — processus accessorius, BRUZELIUS — little or sometimes not at all developed. To this may be added that the 2 nd pair of truncal feet are very long and slender, having in general a very small claw, which however is in one instance absent.

DANA [1]) and SPENCE BATE [2]), who give to this group a wider range, lay stress on the size of the epimera, (coxae, S. BATE), but this is no distinguishing feature, for there are others e. g. *Stegocephalus*, *Pleustes*, *Odius* (*Otus* S. BATE) with equally large or larger epimera. DANA reckons up as belonging to this under-family the genera: *Lysianassa* M. EDWARDS, *Phlias* GUÉRIN-MENEVILLE, *Opis* KRÖYER, *Uristes* DANA, *Anonyx* KRÖYER and *Urothoë* DANA. From these we reject *Phlias*, *Uristes* and *Urothoë*, the two first on the ground that they have no flagellum appendiculare on the upper antennæ, and the last on that of its not having a thick shaft to the upper antennæ, and moreover that it nearly approaches the genus *Phoxus* KRÖYER. SPENCE BATE includes in the sub-family of *Lysianassidae* the genera *Lysianassa*, *Anonyx*, *Pontoporeia* KRÖYER, *Opis*, *Ichnopus* COSTA, *Callisoma* COSTA, *Alibrotus* M. EDWARDS, *Hyale* H. RATHKE, *Phlias* and *Uristes*. Of these we reject *Pontoporeia* on account of the different form of the mandibulæ, and the genera *Alibrotus* and *Hyale* on account of the entirely different construction of the upper antennæ and second pair of feet. The genus *Ichnopus* appears to us identical with that of *Lysianassa*, and as regards *Phlias* and *Uristes* we have already stated our opinion. We therefore include in this sub-family only the genera *Lysianassa*, *Anonyx*, *Callisoma* and *Opis*, to which we add the two new genera *Eurytenes* and *Acidostoma*. In order to illustrate our view of the family *Gammaridae* and the underfamily *Lysianassina*, we adduce here first a tableau of the families included in the suborder *Amphipoda*, and next a similar tableau of the sub-families comprised in the family *Gammaridae*, and, as therewith connected, of the genera within the same family belonging to our-own fauna. We do this the rather since no new synopsis of the kind has appeared since the year 1859, when Doctor BRUZELIUS in Kongl. Wetenskaps-Akademiens Handlingar, (new series) Vol. 3, p. 1. published his excellent paper "Bidrag till kännedom om Skandinaviens *Amphipoda Gammaridea*" (Contributions to the knowledge of the Amphipoda Gammaridea of Scandinavia). Our knowledge of these crustacea has since that time received considerable additions from the labours of Candidate A. BOECK, Professor M. SARS, and the observations we have ourselves had the opportunity of making on the Western Coast of Norway, and we can accordingly now include 36 genera as belonging to our fauna, while BRUZELIUS has only 19. Of these genera 4 are new viz. *Eurytenes*, *Acidostoma*, *Tiron* and *Oediceropsis*, of which genus *Eurytenes*

---

[1]) Explor. Exped. Crustacea. T. II. p. 908.

[2]) Catalogue etc. p. 64.

GENERA:

Fig. 18.

Familiae:

Amphipoda

1. Gammaridae, Dana.
2. Orchestidae, Dana.
3. Corophidae, Dana.
4. Chelonidae, Abbot.
5. Dujardidae, Dana.
6. Darcinidae, Dana.
7. Caprellidae, Dana.
8. Cyamidae, Dana.

Fig. 22.

Species:

Anonyx

1. ampulla (Phipps) Kröyer.
2. longipes, Spence Bate.
3. gulosus, Kröyer.
4. ...., n. sp.
5. pinguis, n. sp.
6. Lundbergianus, n. sp.
7. Boeckii, A. Boeck.
8. nanus, Kröyer.
9. plautus, A. Boeck.
10. ...., A. Boeck.
11. Edwardsii, Kröyer.
12. tumidus, Kröyer.
13. abyssinus, Kröyer.
14. stimulans, A. Boeck.
15. ...., Kröyer.

has been already described, and of the genus *Acidostoma* full details vill be given in the sequel.

The genus *Tiron* [1]) is typified in a species, found by us at Christiansund in Norway at a depth of 30 to 40 fathoms, which we in our public lectures have called *Tiron acanthurus*. n. sp.

Forma capitis ex parte cum eadem gen. *Oediceri* congruit, antennæ superiores vero flagello appendiculari longo sunt præditæ, et pedes trunci 7:mi paris longitudine pedes anteriores æquant, et breves, crassi et unguiferi sunt. Pedes trunci 1:mi et 2:di paris graciles, ungue tamen non flexibili instructi. Segmenta caudalia superne in medion longitudinaliter carinata, carina ad marginem posteriorem segmentorum in aculeum, qui in segmentis 4:to et 5:to magnus est, et adhuc in segmento 6:to observatur, excurrente. Antennæ superiores longitudine pedunculo antennarum inferiorum æquales. Frons aliquanto producta, basin antennarum superiorum obtegens, rostro brevi sed acuto. Oculi rubri. Longitudo circ. 10 millim.

The genus *Oediceropsis* is also typified by a single species, found by us in the sea off Molde in Norway at a depth of 40 or 50 fathoms, which we in our public lectures have called *Oediceropsis brevicornis* n. sp., the upper antennæ being particularly short.

Forma corporis eidem gen. *Oediceri* valde similis, caput tamen rostro caret, et pedes trunci 7:mi paris, qui longum et rectum unguem habent, et longi et graciles sunt, tamen pedibus anterioribus 6:ti paris non duplo — circ. sesqui — longiores sunt. Antennæ superiores non finem articuli penultimi pedunculi antennarum inferiorum assequuntur, et flagello appendiculari carent. Antennæ inferiores magnæ, fere pediformes, articulo penultimo pedunculi ceteris majore et ad apicem infra setam magnam gerente. Oris partes appendiculares et hujus et anterioris speciei structura solita. Pedes trunci 1:mi et 2:di paris forma inter se similes, manu subcheliformi, ovali, carpo postice aliquantum producto. Pedes trunci 3:tii et 4:ti paris parvi et graciles. Segmentum caudale 7:mum integrum et parvum sed laminare. Pedes caudales ultimi ramis duobus angustis, fere æqualibus. Color flavescens; oculi rubescentes, sed parum visibiles. Longitudo circ. 8 millim.

To the genera *Microplax*, *Odius* and *Calliopius* we have given new names instead of the names *Iduna*, *Otus* and *Calliope*, which had already before been given to other animals.

---

[1]) *Teigwr* Proper name.

This being premised we proceed to give an account of such species of the sub-family *Lysianassina* as belong to our Fauna, describing somewhat more in detail those which are new to science or even additions to our own Fauna.

Gen. LYSIANASSA H. M. EDWARDS.

Pedes trunci s. thoracici 1:mi paris manu subcheliformi carentes, ungue non flexibili, segmento 6:to sive manu apicem versus attenuato ibidemque basi unguis vix crassiore. Mandibulae tuberculo molari minimo. Laminae exteriores maxillipedum margine interiore noduloso vel laeviusculo.

We have in Sweden and Norway only 3 species of that genus distinguishable in the following manner.

Lysianassa.	fissum.	Laminæ branchiales	pectinatim plicatæ ...	1. *spinicornis* (A. Boeck).
Segmentum			non plicatæ	2. *Valdi* (Kröyer).
7:mum caudæ ...	non fissum, margine posteriore convexo			3. *Costæ*, M. Edwards.

1. *L. Spinicornis* (A. BOECK).

Ichnopus spinicornis, A. BOECK: Forhandl. ved de Skand. Naturf:s 8:de Möde, 1860, pag. 645.

Antennæ longæ, inferiores superioribus longiores. Segmenta 2:dum et 3:tium pedunculi antennarum superiorum brevissima, et segmentum 1:mum ejusdem pedunculi ad apicem infra aculeo armatum. Flagellum harum antennarum maris circit. 85—100, et feminæ circit. 60—66 articulis brevibus compositum, articulo 1:mo ultimis duobus articulis pedunculi conjunctis longiore, et intus circit. 23 paribus fasciculorum pilorum transversis prædito. Flagellum appendiculare longum, articulis circ. 10. Flagellum antennarum inferiorum articulis circ. 80—120.

Mandibulæ acie obliqua, utrinque denticulo obsoleto munita, processu accessorio carentes. Tuberculum molare parvum, reflexum, acuminatum et pilosum. Palpus magnus, segmento 2:do latiusculo, et 3:tio arcuato et ad latus alterum pectinatim aculeato. Maxillæ 1:mi paris ramo exteriore valido, ad apicem aculeis magnis, ex parte pectinatis, et pilis armato; ramo interiore minore apice pilos duos gerente; et palpo biarticulato, apice truncato, striato et aculeato. Maxillæ 2:di paris ramis angustis et ad apicem aculeatis. Pedes maxillares sive maxillipedes laminis interioribus brevibus ad apicem oblique truncatis et nodulis 2, et setis circ. 5; et laminis exterioribus magnis margine interiore noduloso.

Pedes trunci 1:mi paris segmento 6:to, sive manu, elongato et paullulum arcuato, ungue sat magno et intus fasciculo aculeorum armato. Pedes trunci 2:di paris manu subcheliformi, obovali et setis longis dense obsita. Vesiculæ branchiales pectinatim plicatæ, plicis a rachi media exeuntibus.

Epimera segmenti 3:tii caudæ angulo inferiore et posteriore aculeato. Pedes caudales ultimi ramis elongato-lanceolatis, marginibus exteriore et interiore aculeatis et pilosis. Segmentum 7:mum caudæ ultra medium fissum, laciniis contiguis, obtusis et aculeo ad apicem munitis. Oculi magni, reniformes, fusci. — Longitudo 30—40 millim.

Ad Bergen et Trondhjem in Norvegia accepta, haud frequens.

2. L. Vahli (Kröyer).

Anonyx Vahli, H. Kröyer: Grönlands Amphipoder, pag. 5.
        "   "   Idem: Naturhist. Tidskr. 2 Række, Bd. 1, pag. 599.
        "   "   R. Bruzelius: Skandinaviens Amphipoda Gammaridea; Kongl. Wetensk. Akad:s Handlingar, ny följd, Bd. 3, 1 häftet.

Segmenta 2:dum et 3:tium pedunculi antennarum superiorum brevissima, dimidio segmenti 1:mi breviora. Flagellum appendiculare harum antennarum articulis 5—6. Pedes caudales ultimi ramis latiusculis, et eorum exterior marginibus piliferis. Segmentum ultimum caudæ sive appendix caudalis fere usque ad dimidiam partem fissum, laciniis apice rotundatis. Oculi aterrimi, reniformes. Longitudo 9—20 millim.

Habitat ad oras nostras occidentales a Bergen in Norvegia ad Finmarkiam, rara.

3. L. Costae, H. Milne Edwards.

Lysianassa Costae, H. Milne Edwards: Histoire naturelle des Crustacés, T. III, pag. 21.
        "   "   C. Spence Bate: Catalogue of the specimens of Amphipodous Crustacea in the Collection of the British Museum, pag. 69, tab. 10, fig. 11.
        "   "   Idem & J. O. Westwood: History of British Sessile-Eyed Crustacea, Amphipoda, T. 1, pag. 74.

Lobuli laterales testæ capitis anteriores longe producti. Epimera magna. Epimera segmenti 3:tii caudæ angulo posteriore et inferiore aculeo brevi et superne vergente. Oculi magni, supra approximati, reniformes, fusci. Segmenta 2:dum et 3:tium pedunculi antennarum superiorum longiuscula, una segmento 1:mo longitudine circ. æqualia. Antennæ superiores et inferiores apud feminam longitudine circ. æquales, flagello superiorum pilis longis, et articulis 9—11 composito, articulo 1:mo brevi. Flagellum appendiculare biarticulatum articulo ultimo minimo. Mandibulæ acie utrinque denticulo obsoleto, processu accessorio longo et tenui, tuberculo vel processu molari minuto, fere evanescente, tantummodo lobulum parvum setiferum præbente. Palpus mand. longus. Maxillæ 1:mi paris palpo biarticulato, ad apicem aculeis 5 brevibus, quorum uno mobili; ramo interiore sat magno. Maxillæ 2:di paris ramo interiore latiore, oblongo-ovali. Maxillipedes laminis interioribus magnis, et exterioribus vix apicem articuli 2:di palpi attingentibus, ovatis, apice rotundato et non setifero, margineque interiore læviusculo et vix noduloso. Pedes trunci, 1:mi paris segmento 6:to, sive manu, conico et ungue parvo. Pedes trunci 2:di paris graciles manu fere oblongo-ovali carpoque breviore et minore. Pedes trunci 3:tii et 4:ti paris etiam graciles. Pedescaudales longi, et eorum ultimum par ramis subulatis minimeque setiferis. Segmentum 7:mum caudæ, sive appendix caudalis, integrum, ovale, margine postico leviter convexo et utrinque seta una minima. — Longit. circ. 10 millim. — Ad Christianssund in Norvegia eam haud frequentem invenimus.

2. Gen. EURYTENES nov. gen.

Vide supra!

3. Gen. ANONYX, Kröyer.

Pedes trunci (thoracici) 1:mi paris manu subcheliformi armati, ungue flexibili, margine inferiore manus plus vel minus definito. Mandibulae tuberculo molari mediocri vel magno. Laminae exteriores pedum maxillarium margine interiore plerumque noduloso, raro dentato vel aculeato.

We have on our coasts at least fifteen species of that genus, and of these two are as yet undescribed, one confounded with another species, and one as yet found only on the English coast and in the neighbourhood of the Shetland Isles. In order to facilitate the often difficult work of discriminating the different species, we subjoin a synoptical table of these species, and call attention to such distinguishing marks as seem to us impor-

tant. We further add the accompanying list with such descriptions and re-
marks as the circumstances give rise to.

1. A. AMPULLA (Phipps); Kröyer.

Anonyx ampulla, H. Kröyer: Naturhist. Tidsskr. 2 Række, 1 Bd. pag. 578.

"   "   R. Bruzelius: Skandinaviens Amphipoda Gammaridea, pag.
39; Wetensk. Akad:s Handl., ny följd, Bd. 3 1859.

This species does not appear in Spence Bate's and J. O. Westwood's "British Sessile-eyed Crustacea." The species there introduced
under this name is a totally different one, as will presently be shown.

2. A. LONGIPES. Spence Bate.

Anonyx longipes, C. Spence Bate: Catalogue of the specimens of Amphipodous Crustacea in the Collection of the British Museum,
pag. 79, pl. XIII, fig. 4. — Femina.

"   "   C. Spence Bate & J. O. Westwood: History of British
Sessile-Eyed Crustacea, T. I, pag. 113. — Femina.

"   *ampulla*, C. Spence Bate: Catalogue etc., pag 79, pl. XIII, fig.
5. — Mas.

"   "   C. Spence Bate & J. O. Westwood: History etc. pag.
116. — Mas.

Descr. Longitudo corp. 12—13 millim. Forma corporis gracilis et
elongata, epimeris mediocribus, capite parvo et ejus lobulis lateralibus acutis, segmento 3:tio caudæ postice gibbo, ejusque angulis lateralibus posterioribus (fig. 30, *a*) in aculeum longum et recurvum productis. Pedes trunci
longi et graciles.

Antennæ superiores *feminæ* (fig. 23) segmentis 2:do et 3:tio pedunculi brevissimis, flagelli articulis circ. 15, et flagelli appendicularis articulis 5. Antennæ inferiores superioribus fere longitudine æquales. Antennæ
superiores *maris* iisdem feminæ longiores, et ejus antennæ inferiores flagello
gracillimo et longissimo, ut partem posteriorem caudæ interdum asse-
quantur.

Labrum (Fig. 24) parte superiore (*a*) in longum acumen durum, com-
pressum et recurvum porrecta, et infra ad ejus basin lobulis duobus mol-
libus (*b, b*) basin prope infra hispidis. Labium (*c, c*) ramis duobus ad apicem setiferis confectum.

Mandibularum (fig. 25) acies tantummodo uno denticulo. Processus accessorius forma aculei magni et arcuati distinctus, et tuberculum molare magnum excavatum et hispidum aculeis brevissimis.

Maxillæ 1:mi paris (fig. 26) forma solita, ramo interiore et minore ad apicem duas setas gerente, et ramo exteriore crasso apiceque circ. 7—8 dentibus magnis et serratis armato. Palpus ad apicem denticulis brevibus circ. 8. — Maxillæ 2:di paris ramis ambo fere latitudine æqualibus.

Maxillipedes laminis interioribus medium laminarum exteriorum assequentibus, et hæ laminæ (enter.) ad marginem interiorem nodulis confertis præditæ, ad apicem vero aculeis carentes.

Pedes trunci 1:mi paris (fig. 27) minus robusti, segmento 3:tio dimidio segmenti 2:di multo breviore. Manus rectangularis, carpo fere aequalis, ungue parvo dente uno prope apicem intus armato. — Pedes 2:di paris (fig. 28) gracillimi, segmento 3:tio dimidio segmenti 2:di fere æquali. Manus oblongus, fere rectangularis, carpo parum brevior sed latior, et margine posteriore convexo, ungue minuto, intus aculeato.

Pedes trunci trium parium posteriorum longi et graciles ungue longo et vix arcuato. — Pedes caudales ultimi (fig. 29) ramis fere aequalibus, lanceolatis, et aculeatis, et ad marginem interiorem setiferis.

Segmentum 7:mum caudæ sive appendix caudalis (fig. 31) supra utrinque aculeis tribus, et fissura basin propius incipiente marginibusque divergentibus. Laciniæ ad apicem 1—3 aculeos gerentes.

Color flavido-albus. Oculi rubri.

Ad Haugesund, Molde et Christianssund in Norvegia hanc speciem non infrequentem invenimus, et Doctor G. LINDSTRÖM eam ad Farsund in eadem terra accepit; in profunditate 15—60 orgyiarum, et plerumque in fundo arenoso. Antea tantummodo in Anglia accepta.

3. A. GULOSUS. KRÖYER.

Anonyx gulosus, H. KRÖYER: Naturhist. Tidskr. 2 Række, 1 Bd, pag. 611.

    „   *norvegicus*, LILLJEBORG: Öfvers. af Kongl. Wetensk. Akademiens Förh. 1851, pag. 22.

    „   „   R. BRUZELIUS Skandinaviens Amphipoda Gammaridea pag. 44.

    „   *Holbölli*, SPENCE BATE AND WESTWOOD. British Sessile-Eyed Crustacea, T. 1, pag. 104.

This species is easily recognized by the following characteristics. The 1st pair of feet have the 3rd joint as long as or longer than half of the 2nd; the claw is armed at the inner edge with a strong tooth; the edge of the hand, to which the claw is attached is furnished with a row of extremely fine spines arranged like the teeth of a comb, within which are scantily set bristles; and last the 3rd tail-segment has the lower back angle but little drawn out, but acute. The processus accessorius of the mandibula is particularly prominent, and on one side provided with teeth.

In very young individuals the 3rd joint of the 1st pair of feet is shorter than half of the second, and they closely approach the *A. nanoides*, from which however they may be distinguished by the abovementioned pair of feet beeing longer and slenderer, and by the fore and back borders of the hands being somewhat curved but not convergent, as in the latter species. The carpus of the 2nd pair of feet is not quite double as long as the hand.

This species occurs on our west coast from Bohuslän to Finmarken, and is extended northward to Greenland and southward to England.

4. A. NANOIDES, n. sp.

It is probably this species that R. Bruzelius (l. c.) has described under the name of *Anonyx nanus* Kröyer with a note of interrogation. In his description he has omitted the minute denticle on the inner side of the claw of the 1st pair of feet.

Descr. Minor; longitudo circ. 5—6 millim. Corporis forma sat obesa, tamen compressa, epimeris magnis, et pedibus brevibus, et unguibus pedum trunci posteriorum arcuatis. Segmentum 3:tium caudae angulis posterioribus et inferioribus (fig. 34 a) recurvis sed minus acutis.

Antennae superiores inferioribus paullulum breviores, segmentis 2:do et 3:o pedunculi brevissimis. Flagellum articulis 10, quorum primus maximus, fere 3:tiae parti flagelli aequalis. Flagellum appendiculare articulo 1:mo flagelli longius, circ. finem articuli 5:ti assequens, articulis 6. Antennae inferiores articulis flagelli circ. 20. Maxillipedes laminis exterioribus ad medium circiter articuli 3:tii palpi porrectis, oblongo-ovatis, apice obtuse angulato, margine exteriore apicem propius eroso ibique seta minore, margineque interiore noduloso, nodulis minimis et paucis. Laminae interiores ad medium exteriorum extensae.

Pedes trunci 1:mi paris (fig. 32) sat robusti, segmento 3:tio dimidio segmenti 2:di breviore, manu rectangulari, apicem versus parum angustiore, longitudine carpo circ. æquali. Unguis crassus et brevis, intus aculeo et setis.

Pedes trunci 2:di paris gracillimi, manu (fig. 33) ovali, longitudine dimidia carpi, et angulo inferiore et posteriore producto et acuto.

Rami pedum caudalium ultimorum aculeati non vero setiferi, exterior interiore longior.

Oculi rubri.

Tantummodo specimen unum junius ad Molde in Norvegia accepi.

5. A. PUMILUS, n. sp.

Descr. Minor; longitudo circ. 5 millim. Forma corporis minus obesa quam apud præcedentem, epimeris et pedibus mediocribus, dorso vero latinsculo. Ungues pedum trunci posteriorum longi et parum arcuati. Segmentum 3:tium caudæ angulis posterioribus et inferioribus (fig. 41) productis, acuminatis et recurvis.

Antennæ superiores (fig. 35) inferioribus parum breviores, segmentis 2:do et 3:tio pedunculi brevissimis. Flagellum articulis 7, quorum 1:mus ceteris major est. Flagellum appendiculare articulis 3, ad medium flagelli porrectum. — Antennæ inferiores articulis flagelli 8.

Mandibulæ (fig. 36) acie utrinque dente munita, processu accessorio et tuberculo molari distinctis. — Pedes maxillares laminis exterioribus oblongo-ovatis non apicem articuli 2:di palpi attingentibus, ad apicem aculeos setiformes 5 gerentibus, margine interiore noduloso, nodulis minimis paucis (6—7) et discretis. Laminæ interiores vix dimidium lam. exteriorum attingentes, ad apicem dentibus 3—4, et setis 3.

Pedes trunci 1:mi paris robusti, segmento 3:tio dimidio 2:di multo breviore, et manu (fig. 37) pyramidata vel triangulari, et margine palmæ vix definito. Unguis magnus, intus denticulo minimo et setis duabus vel tribus. — Pedes trunci 2:di paris parum graciles, manu (fig. 38 ovali et carpo breviore, angulo posteriore et inferiore fere recto, ungueque sat magno.

Pedes caudales ultimi (fig. 39) ramis subulatis et setis carentibus, exteriore longiore.

Segmentum caudæ 7:mum (fig. 40) sat elongatum, profunde — ultra medium — fissum, laciniis contiguis, ad apicem emarginatis, ibique aculeum gerentibus.

Color dilute ruber. — Oculi obsoleti.

Tantummodo specimen unum ad Molde in Norvegia in profundo 40—50 orgyiarum et fundo argillaceo inveni.

6. A. BRACHYCERCUS, n. sp.

Descr. Minimus; longitudo 4 millim. Forma corporis valde crassa et brevis, epimeris magnis, et pedibus brevibus et robustis, unguibus arcuatis. Segmentum 3:tium caudæ angulis posterioribus et inferioribus (fig. 49) productis, acutis et recurvis.

Antennæ breves et crassæ, superiores et inferiores longitudine circ. æquales; superiores (fig. 42) segmentis 2:do et 3:o pedunculi brevissimis, flagelli articulis 4, quorum 1:mo maximo. Flagellum appendiculare biarticulatum, articulo 1:mo magno, et 2:do minimo; — inferiores flagelli articulis 4, quorum 1:mus non multum ab articulo ultimo pedunculi diversus est.

Mandibulæ (fig. 43) acie utrinque dente obsoleto, processu accessorio distincto, et tuberculo molari elongato et compresso, et subtilissime hispido, nulli vero aculei inter hoc et processum accessorium adsunt.

Maxillæ 1:mi paris forma solita, ramo interiore bisetoso. — Maxillæ 2:di paris ramo interiore fere latiore sed breviore.

Maxillipedes (fig. 44) laminis interioribus (*a*) elongatis, ad medium laminarum exteriorum porrectis, ad apicem nodulis 3 et setis 3. Laminæ exteriores magnæ, ultra medium articuli 3:tii palpi extensæ, ad marginem interiorem tantummodo apicem propius nodulosæ, nodulis discretis 4, et ad marginem exteriorem setam unam et pilos minimos gerentes.

Pedes trunci 1:mi paris breves et robusti, segmento 3:tio dimidiæ segmenti 2:di longitudini circ. æquali, et manu (fig. 45) carpo longiore, versus apicem inferiorem angustiore, marginibusque anteriore et posteriore arcuatis. Unguis magnus, intus dente uno et setis tribus instructus. — Pedes trunci 2:di paris (fig. 46) sat robusti, segmento 2:do sinuato, et 3:tio dimidia longitudine segmenti 2:di fere longiore. Manus carpo brevior, oblongo-ovalis, angulo inferiore et posteriore acuto, ungue crasso et intus dentato. — Pedes trunci parium trium posteriorum segmento 2:do sequentibus segmentis conjunctis multo longiore. — Pedes caudales ultimi (fig. 47) breves et crassi, ramo exteriore longiore et interiore apice minutissime bifido, et ramis ambo aculeis et setis carentibus.

Segmentum ultimum caudæ (fig. 48) late ovatum, ad medium circ. fissum, laciniis ad apicem aculeum gerentibus.

Oculi rubri.

Specimen unum ad Grip juxta Christianssund in Norvegia e profundo 20—30 orgyiarum cepi.

7. A. BRUZELII, A. BOECK.

Anonyx Bruzelii, AXEL BOECK: Forhandlinger ved de Skandinaviske Natur-forskeres 8:de Möde, 1860 (tr. 1861) pag. 643.

Of this species we have no other knowledge than what is derived from BOECK'S above-cited description, having never met with a specimen. It was found by the author referred to on the west coast of Norway. As regards the construction of the first pair of feet it somewhat approaches *A. gulosus;* nevertheless these feet are a little longer and slenderer than in that species, and it is not stated that the claw is furnished with any tooth on the inner side. The external lamina of the maxillipeds has only a few knobs on its inner border, whereas the *A. gulosus* has many.

8. A. NANUS, KRÖYER.

Anonyx nanus, H. KRÖYER: Naturhistorisk Tidsskr. 2 Række, 2 Bd. pag. 30.

Distinguitur: Anguli posteriores et inferiores segmenti 3:tii caudæ obtusi. Flagellum appendiculare anteun. super. triarticulatus, ad finem ar-ticuli 3:tii flagelli porrectum, articulo 1:mo ceteris pluries longiore. Arti-culus 1:mus flagelli reliquis conjunctis longitudine æqualis. Maxillipedum laminæ interiores ad marginem apicalem dentibus obtusis tribus et setis dua-bus. Laminæ eorum exteriores ad marginem interiorem nodulis, sive den-tibus obtusis confertis. Pedes trunci 1:mi paris breves et robusti, segmento 3:tio dimidia longitudine segm. 2:di breviore, manu carpo longitudine æquali, rectangulari, marginibus anteriore et posteriore arcuatis, et margine infe-riore truncato; ungue crasso et intus dente sat valido armato.

Pedum caudalium ultimorum ramus exterior ad marginem interiorem setis ciliatis longis circ. 10 instructus, et ramus interior apice bicuspide. Segmentum 7:mum caudæ ultra medium fissum, fissura aperta. Longit. circ. 5 m. m.

Oculi rubri.

A KRÖYER in Kattegat ad Hornbæk (parte australi), a Doctore G. LINDSTRÖM ad Farsund in Norvegia acceptus.

9. A. PINGUIS, A. BOECK.

Anonyx pinguis, AXEL BOECK: Forhandl: ved de Skand. Naturf:s 8:de Möde, 1860 (tr 1861), pag. 642.

This animal is also known to us only by the description cited. It is found on the west coast of Norway. In the form of the 7th tail-segment, which is divided only half-way, it approaches the above described *A. brachycercus*, as also probably in a thick and stout form of body, but is easily distinguished from it by having the lower back angles of the 3rd caudal segment rounded off. The flagellum of the upper antennae has 20 joints and the flagellum appendiculare 4, of which the first is long, with teeth on the under side. The first pair of feet have the hand longer than the carpus, cut off at right angles at the lower end.

10. A. SERRATUS, A. BOECK.

Anonyx serratus, AXEL BOECK: Forhandl ved de Skand. Naturf:s 8:de Möde, 1860, pag. 641.

  „   *Edwardsii*, C. SPENCE BATE: Catalogue etc. pag. 73, Pl. XI, fig. 5.

  „   „   SPENCE BATE AND J. O. WESTWOOD: British Sessile-Eyed Crustacea, T. I, pag. 94.

Easily distinguished from all our other species of the genus *Anonyx* by the back border of the 3rd caudalsegment's epimera being saw-toothed, (fig. 50) and by the lower angles of these epimera being rounded off. The back borders of the 1st and 2nd caudalsegments are also saw-toothed.

Forma corporis obesa, epimeris magnis, pedibus gracilibus non vero longis, unguibus arcuatis. Longitudo circ. 7 millim.

Antennæ superiores inferioribus breviores, flagello 9, et flagello appendiculari 5 articulis.

Mandibularum acies altero dente laterali plane obsoleto, et processu accessorio distincto et ad latus alterum dentato. — Maxillarum 1:mi paris ramus interior elongatus, ultra medium rami exterioris porrectus, apiceque bisetoso, palpus ad apicem truncatum dentibus 6, et aculeo uno. — Maxillæ 2:di paris ramo exteriore interiore longiore et latiore. — Maxillipedes s. pedes maxillares laminis interioribus ad medum laminarum exteriorum porrectis, et ad apicem subsinuatum tuberculis tribus et setis ciliatis tribus; laminis exterioribus ad finem articuli 2:di palpi extensis, et ad marginem interiorem confertim nodulosis.

Pedes trunci 1:mi paris breves et robusti, segmento 3:tio dimidia longitudine segmenti 2:di multo breviore. Manus carpo longior, rectangularis, marginibus anteriore et posteriore arcuatis, et margine inferiore sive palmæ crenulato. Unguis crassus et brevis intus denticulo minimo. — Pedes trunci 2:di paris forma solita, manu carpo breviore et angustiore, subsemilunari, hirsutissima, angulo posteriore et inferiore producto et acuto, ungue minimo intus dentato. — Pedes caudales ultimi ramis lanceolatis et aculeatis non vero setiferis, exteriore longiore.

Segmentum caudæ 7:mum usque ad sed non ultra medium fissum, fissura aperta. Laciniæ ad apicem aculeum unum, et in latere superiore aculeos tres gerentes.

Ad Grip juxta Christianssund in Norvegia specimina duo e 20—30 orgyarum profundo et fundo arenoso accepi.

11. A. EDWARDSII, KRÖYER.

Anonyx Edwardsii, H. KRÖYER: Naturhist. Tidsskr. 2 Række, 2 Bd. pag. 1.
    „   „   R. BRUZELIUS: Skandinaviens Amphipoda Gammaridea, pag. 46.

This species also we have never had an opportunity of examining, and accordingly know it only by the descriptions given by KRÖYER and BRUZELIUS. According to the last named writer it is seldom met with on our western coasts from Bohuslän to Finmarken. It is distinguished by the form of the 7:th caudal-segment, which is short and broad, and has at the back border a very shallow but clearly visible notch; it has also a property in common only with the following species, viz. that the claw of the first pair of feet has on the inner side a tooth, within which is a row of very fine saw-teeth.

12. A. LITORALIS, KRÖYER.

Anonyx litoralis, H. KRÖYER: Naturhist. Tidsskr. 2 Række, 1 B. pag. 621.
    „   „   R. BRUZELIUS: Skandinaviens Amphipoda Gammaridea, pag. 46.

This species, like the preceeding, is distinguished by the form of the last caudal-segment, which is unforked, and in the back border has only a slight indication of inward curvature. It also has a tooth on the inner side of the claw of 1:st pair of feet, and inside that a row of fine saw-teeth, but both these last and the tooth itself are larger than in the preceeding species.

On our coasts it is confined to the extreme north. M:r Doct. TH. FRIES has brought home & presented to the University Zoological Museum a specimen taken by him on the coast of Warangartjord.

Longit. 14—15 millim. Segmentum 3:tium caudae angulis inferioribus et posterioribus acutis, non vero productis. Mandibulæ acie subtilissime crenulata, utrinque dente sat valido, processu accessorio distincto, solito modo stiliformi, tuberculo molari mediocri denticulato et hispido. — Maxillæ 1:mi paris ramo interiore parvo, rotundato, setis duabus, et palpo ad apicem aculeis quinque. — Maxillæ 2:di paris ramo exteriore interiore fere duplo majore. — Maxillipedes laminis interioribus brevibus, ad apicem tuberculis tribus et setis duabus vel tribus; laminis exterioribus etiam brevibus, non apicem articuli 2:di palpi assequentibus, margine interiore noduloso, nodulis discretis (circ. 10), et ad marginem exteriorem prope apicem aculeo mobili. — Pedes trunci 1:mi paris brevissimi et robustissimi, manu fere quadrangulari, infra oblique truncata. Oculi rubri, ovato-reniformes.

13. A. HOLBÖLLII, KRÖYER.

Anonyx Holböllii, H. KRÖYER: Naturhist. Tidsskr. 2 Række, 2 Bd. pag. 8.
" " R. BRUZELIUS: Skandinaviens Amphipoda Gammaridea, pag. 43.
" denticulatus, C. SPENCE BATE Catalogue etc. pag. 74, pl. 12, fig. 2. — Mas.
" " C. SPENCE BATE AND WESTWOOD: British Sessile-Eyed Crustacea. T. 1. pag. 104. — Mas.

This species is distinguished from all our other species by having the maxillipeds' outer laminae, which are crescent-shaped, furnished on the inner margin with thickly set, comb-like, long, sharp teeth, 17 to 20 in number, and by the hand of the 1st pair of feet, which is oblong-oval, and has the lower back angle obliquely rounded off, and is furnished with a smooth and peculiarly long claw, which when pressed in reaches with its point back to the middle of the hand. It might therefore be veury well considered as the type of a separate genus. It is also remarkable for the 3rd caudal-segment's lower and back angles, which are carried out into a very, long sharp point bent upwards, and for the mandibulae which have the cutting or eggbearing end very small and the tuberculum molare very large hard and prominent. The 1st pair of maxillae have no side-teeth on the large spines at the end of the outer branch, and their palp has a great number of denticles at the point. The second pair of maxillae have the branches very broad. The flagellum appendiculare of the upper antennae has 3 joints, with the 1ˢ joint longer than the other two put together, and the point always turned upward. The lower antennae are in both sexes, but especially in the male, considerably longer than the upper. The claw of the back truncal feet is long and but slightly curved. We have found the body's length 14 millim.

It is met with on our western coasts form Bohuslän to Finmarken, an in one or two places, as for example Haugesund and Molde in Norway we have found it not uncommon, where the bottom is sandy, and at a depth of 12 to 50 fathoms.

14. A. OBTUSIFRONS, A. BOECK.

Anonyx Obtusifrons, AXEL BOECK: Forhandl. ved de Skand. Naturf:s 8:de Möde, 1860, pag. 643.

This species is known to me only by BOECK'S description. The flagellum of the upper antennae has 8 joints, of which the first is as long as all the rest together. The first joint of the flagellum appendiculare is particularly long and provided with several spines on the lower side. The exterior laminae of the maxillipeds have some few scattered coarse teeth on the inner margin. The 3ʳᵈ caudal segment has its lower and back angles drawn out into a long hook or point bent upwards. &c. It is taken on the western coast of Norway.

15. A. TUMIDUS, KRÖYER.

Anonyx tumidus, H. KRÖYER: Naturhist. Tidskr. 2 Række, 2 Bd. pag. 16.
" " R. BRUZELIUS: Skandinaviens Amphipoda Gammaridea, pag. 41.

This species is by the nature of the mouth's appendages, by the form of the hand belonging to the first pair of feet, and by the peculiarity of its habits, so distinguished from every other species of the same genus, that it might very well be considered as the type of a distinct genus. The mandibulae are remarkably small, have the egg-bearing end very small and both side teeth exceedingly small, and are without processus accessorius. The tuberculum molare is very large but thin, brought up to a point and destitute of bristles. The 1ˢ pair of maxillae are short and have both branches, especially the outer, very broad. The inner branch has at its termination 5 coarse ciliated bristles, and the outer has a great many spines. The palp has the usual form. The 2ⁿᵈ pair of maxillae, which are also short, have the inner branch very broad, and the outer much narrower. The maxillipeds (fig. 51) are also short, but have the laminae exteriores very large, and reaching about to the end of the 2ⁿᵈ joint of the palp. The inner laminæ are wery short, armed with coarse ciliated bristles at the end and inner side. The exterior laminae have the internal margin almost smooth, but immediately within the edge is a row of about 7 short spines, directed forwards, the points of which reach beyond the edge of the laminæ, by which this latter shows itself to be thinly set with spines. At the point they have a long spine and beyond that three bristles. The hands of the first pair of feet approach in form those of the genus *Lysianassa*, tapering towards the point, almost conical, and the palm-edge not clearly defined. But the claw is moveable and in some measure doubled back upon the posterior edge of the hand. The whole back edge of the hand is furnished with small spines, and in front of these are a few (5) of larger dimensions. The claw is not, as KRÖYER states, divided at the point, but has however on the inner side an almost invisible prickle. The branches of the last pair of caudal-feet are distinguished by having, like those of the genus *Hyperia*, fine sawteeth, the outer branch only on the inner margin, but the inner branch on both margins.

It is found in the branchial-sack of *Ascidiæ* on our western coast from the southern part of the Kattegat at least up to Christianssund in Norway.

4. Gen. CALLISOMA, A. COSTA.

Cum genere Anonycis maxima ex parte congruens, distinguitur tamen: Pedes trunci 1:mi paris iisdem 2:di paris non crassiores, interdum graciliores, sed longiores, ungue obsoleto vel absente. Ramus interior maxillarum 1:mi paris setis ciliatis sat multis praeditus. — Laminae exteriores maxillipedum margine interiore aculeato. Aculei ad apicem palpi maxillarum 1:mi paris bifurcati.

Of this genus 4 species are known, two from Naples (*Callis. Hopei* and *punctatum* A. COSTA), 1 from England (*Callis. crenata*. S. BATE), and one from Sweden and Norway.

1. C. KRÖYERI (BRUZELIUS).

Anonyx Kröyeri. R. BRUZELIUS: Skandinaviens Amphipoda Gammaridea, pag. 45, tab. II, fig. 7

Callisoma   „   C. SPENCE BATE: Catalogue etc. pag. 371.

The 1st pair of truncal-feet are long and slender, longer than the 2nd, and their hands have a very small and rudimentary claw, concealed by long bristles, on the back border above the lower and back angle. The hand of the 2nd pair of truncal feet has the lower and back corner drawn out so as to be almost cheliform. The upper antennae are shorter than the lower; the 3rd caudal-segment's lower and back corners are rounded off; and the 7th caudal-segment deeply cloven, &c.

According to BRUZELIUS this species is to be met with on our western coasts from Bohuslän to Finmarken.

5. Gen. ACIDOSTOMA. n. gen. [1])

Forma corporis et antennarum cum genere Anonycis congruit, oris partes appendiculares tamen plane diversae. Labii rami laterales angusti. Mandibulae processu accessorio, maxillae 1:mi paris palpo, et palpus maxillipedum ungue carentes, et hae partes oris conjunctim acumen productum praebent. Pedes trunci 1:mi paris robusti, manu prehensili. Pedes 2:di paris graciles, ungue carentes.

Of this genus we know of only one species, namely:

1. ACIDOSTOMA OBESUM (SPENCE BATE).

Anonyx obesus, C. SPENCE BATE: Catalogue etc. pag. 74.
      „   „   C. SPENCE BATE & J. O. WESTWOOD: British Sissile-Eyed Crustacea, T. I, p. 98.

Descr. Corporis forma (fig. 53) obesa, dorso latiusculo et rotundato, epimeris magnis, et pedibus brevibus et robustis, unguibus parum arcuatis, angulis posterioribus et inferioribus segmenti 3:tii caudae obtusis. Longitudo circ. 5 millim. — Color ruber; oculi rotundati, fusci.

Caput parvum, lobi laterales parum producti. Antennae superiores (fig. 54) pedunculi segmentis 2:do et 3:tio brevibus, flagello articulis circ. 7 quorum primo brevissimo; flagelloque appendiculari longitudine flagello fere aequali, articulis 5. — Antennae inferiores longitudine superioribus circ. aequales, flagelli articulis 7.

Labrum (fig. 55, *a*) vomeriforme, et labii partes laterales sive rami angusti (*b, b*), ad apicem acuminati et intus hispidi. Mandibulae (fig. 56) elon-

---

[1]) From ἀκίς a point and στόμα mouth, because the mouth and its appendages form a long projecting point.

gatæ, processu accessorio carentes, acie utrinque denticulo minutissimo. Tuberculum molare (a) non postice definitum. Palpus longus et gracilis, segmento 2:do ceteris longiore, et segmento 3:tio ad apicem setifero. — Maxillæ 1:mi paris (fig. 57) palpo carentes, angustæ, ramo exteriore (a) et majore ad apicem dentibus curvatis et partim serratis circ. 8 armato, ramo interiore minore ad apicem setas paucas gerente. — Maxillæ 2:di paris (fig. 58) minores et adhuc angustiores, ramo exteriore interiore longiore, et ambo ad apicem setiferis. — Maxillipedes (fig. 59) laminis interioribus mediocribus, ad apicem setis 3—4, et laminis exterioribus maximis, fere semilunaribus, marginibusque lævibus, interioribus tantum apicem versus nodulis minutissimis et obsoletis paucis instructis. Palpus ungue carens, laminæ exteriori longitudine circ. æqualis, articulis elongatis, sed eorum 4:to brevissimo.

Pedes trunci 1:mi paris (fig. 60) breves et robusti, segmento 3:tio dimidia longitudine segmenti 2:di breviore. Manus carpo circ. æqualis, conica, margine anteriore arcuato et posteriore recto et minutissime hispido, prætereaque setis majoribus. Unguis flexibilis, arcuatus et lævis. — Pedes trunci 2:di paris (fig. 61) iisdem 1:mi paris graciliores et longiores, manu valde hispida, oblonga, fere æquilata, parum arcuata et carpo breviore et angustiore, apice obtuso et ungue carente. — Pedes 3:tii et 4:ti paris (fig. 62, pes 3:tii paris) ungue articulo unguifero paullulum breviore. — Pedes trunci trium parium posteriorum inter se fere eadem forma, breves et lati (fig. 63, pes 7:mi paris), segmento 2:do maximo et sequentibus conjunctis longitudine fere æquali, postice infra serrato et antice aculeato; unguis validus et modice arcuatus. Pedes 5:ti et 6:ti paris segmento 2:do eodem pedum 7:mi paris paullulum breviore. — Vesiculæ branchiales simplices.

Pedes caudales ultimi (fig. 64) ramis lanceolatis, exteriore angustiore et longiore, apiceque tuberculo minimo.

Segmentum 7:mum caudæ (fig. 65) latum, fere rotundatum, ultra medium fissum, laciniis apice obtuso et aculeo brevissimo instructo.

Ad Molde in Norvegia e profundo 30—40 orgyiarum et fundo argillaceo hanc speciem haud frequentem invenimus. Doctor LINDSTRÖM eam ad Farsund in Norvegia et in Bahusia accepit.

EXPLICATIO FIGURARUM.

Tabula I.

Eurytenes magellanicus.

Fig. 1. Animal, magnitudine naturali. *b'*, segmentum 1:mum pedunculi antennæ inferioris.

" 2. Caput cum antennis, a latere dextro visum. *b*, segmentum 1:mum pedunculi antennæ inferioris.

" 3. Caput, visum a latere inferiore. *a, a,* antennæ superiores. *b, b,* antennæ inferiores. *c, c,* labrum. *d, d,* mandibulæ. d', d', palpi mandibularum. *g, g,* segmenta 1:ma truncorum pedam maxillarium sive maxillipedum. *g', g',* laminæ exteriores maxillipedum, et *g'', g''* eorum palpi.

" 4. Labrum, *a,* et labium, *b,* a latere sinistro visa.

" 5. *a,* labrum. *b, b,* rami ambo labii.

" 5c. Labium (rami ambo) a latere superiore visum.

" 6. Mandibula sinistra, a latere interiore visa. *a,* acies. *b,* tuberculum molare. *c,* processus lateralis. *d,* palpus.

" 7. Mandibula eadem, a latere exteriore visa, eodem modo signata.

" 8. Maxilla 1:mi paris. *a & a'* ramus exterior sive truncus. *b,* ramus interior. *c,* palpus.

" 9. Maxilla 2:di paris. *a,* ramus exterior. *b,* ramus interior.

Tabula II.

Eurytenes magellanicus.

Fig. 10. Pedes maxillares sive maxillipedes. *a, a,* segmenta 1:ma truncorum. *b, b,* segmenta 2:da corum. *b',* laminæ exteriores. *c, c,* palpi.

" 11. Laminæ interiores maxillipedum.

" 12. Pars Laminæ exterioris corum cum margine interiore.

" 13. Pes dexter 1:mi paris ped. trunci sive thoracicorum. *a & 1,* segmentum 1:mum. 2—6 segmenta 2:dum—6:tum.

" 14. Pes dexter trunci 2:di paris. *a & 1,* segmentum 1:mum, *b,* lamina matricalis sive capsularis. *c,* vesicula branchialis.

Fig. 15.   Pes dexter trunei 3:tii paris.
,,   16.   Pes dexter trunei 6:ti paris. 1 & 2, segmenta 1:mum & 2:dum.
,,   17.   Vesicula branchialis pedis trunci dextri 6:ti paris. *a*, truncus.
,,   18.   Pes caudalis dexter 1:mi paris. *b, b*, rami.

Tabula III.

Fig. 19—22. Eurytenes magellanicus.

Fig. 19.   Pes caudalis dexter 4:ti paris. *a*, ramus exterior. *b*, ramus interior.
,,   20.   Pes caudalis dexter 6:te paris. *a*, ramus exterior. *b*, ramus interior.
,,   21.   Segmentum 7:mum caudæ sive appendix caudalis.
,,   22.   Epimerum dextrum segmenti 3:tii caudæ.

Fig. 23—31. Anonyx longipes.

Fig. 23.   Antenna superior.
,,   24.   *a & b, b*, labrum; *c, c*, labium, a latere dextro visa.
,,   25.   Mandibula.
,,   26.   Maxilla 1:mi paris.
,,   27.   Segmenta ultima pedis trunci 1:mi paris.
,,   28.   Segmenta ultima pedis trunci 2:di paris.
,,   29.   Pes caudalis 6:ti paris sinister. *a & b*, rami exterior et interior
,,   30.   Epimerum segmenti 3:tii caudæ.
,,   31.   Segmentum 7:mum caudæ.

Fig. 32—34. Anonyx nanoides.

Fig. 32.   Pes trunci 1:mi paris.
,,   33.   Pes trunci 2:di paris.
,,   34.   Epimerum segmenti 3:tii caudæ.

Tabula IV.

Fig. 35—41. Anonyx pumilus

Fig. 35.   Antenna superior.
,,   36.   Mandibula.
,,   37.   Segmenta ultima pedis trunci 1:mi paris.
,,   38.   Segmenta ultima pedis trunci 2:di paris.
,,   39.   Pes caudalis 6:ti paris. *a & b*, rami exterior & interior.
,,   40.   Segmentum 7:mum caudæ.
,,   41.   Epimerum segmenti 3:ti caudæ.

Fig. 42—49. Anonyx brachycercus.

Fig. 42.   Antenna superior.
,,   43.   Mandibula.
,,   44.   Pes maxillaris. *a*, lamina interior. *b*, lamina exterior.
,,   45.   Segmenta ultima pedis trunci 1:mi paris.

38

Fig. 46. Pes trunci 2:di paris
„ 47. Pes caudalis 6:ti paris. *a*, ramus exterior.
„ 48. Segmentum 7:mum caudæ.
„ 49. Epimerum segmenti 3:tii caudæ.

Fig. 50. Anonyx serratus

Fig. 50. Epimerum segmenti 3:tii caudæ.

Fig. 51. Anonyx tumidus.

Fig. 51. Pes maxillaris. *a*, lamina interior. *b*, lamina exterior.

Fig. 52. Anonyx ampulla.

Fig. 52. Mandibula. *a*, processus accessorius. *b*, tuberculum molare. *c*, palpus.

Tabula V.

Acidostoma obesum.

Fig. 53. Animal a latere dextro visum.
„ 54. Antenna superior.
„ 55. *a*, labrum. *b, b,* rami labii.
„ 56. Mandibula. *a*, tuberculum molare.
„ 57. Maxilla 1:mi paris. *a & b*, rami exterior & interior.
„ 58. Maxilla 2:di paris. *a & b*, rami exterior & interior.
„ 59. Maxillipedes.
„ 60. Pes trunci 1:mi paris.
„ 61. Pes trunci 2:di paris. *a*, lamina matricalis.
„ 62. Pes trunci 3:tii paris.
„ 63. Pes trunci 7:mi paris.
„ 64. Pes caudalis 6:ti paris. *a*, ramus exterior.
„ 65. Segmentum 7:mum caudæ.

Eurytenes magellanicus

Pl. II

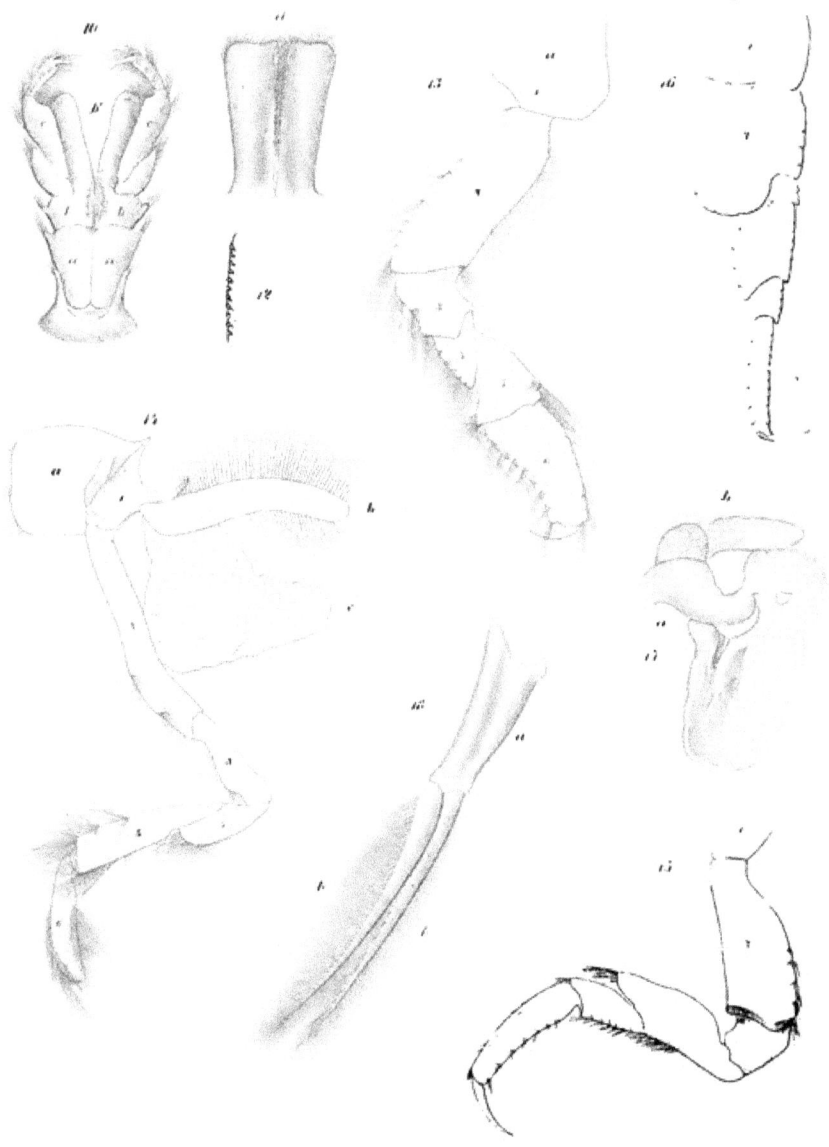

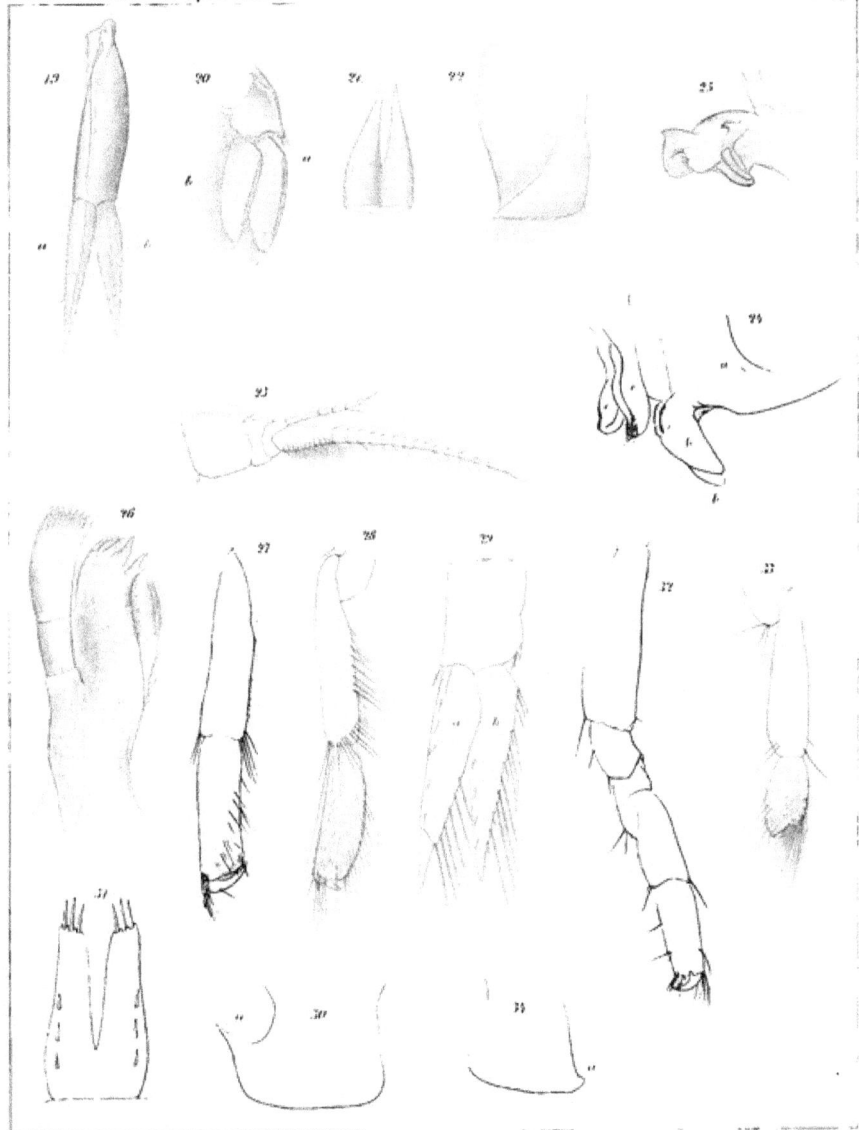

Fig 19-22 Eurytenes magellanicus. Fig 25-51 Anonyx longipes
Fig 52-54 Anonyx nanoides.

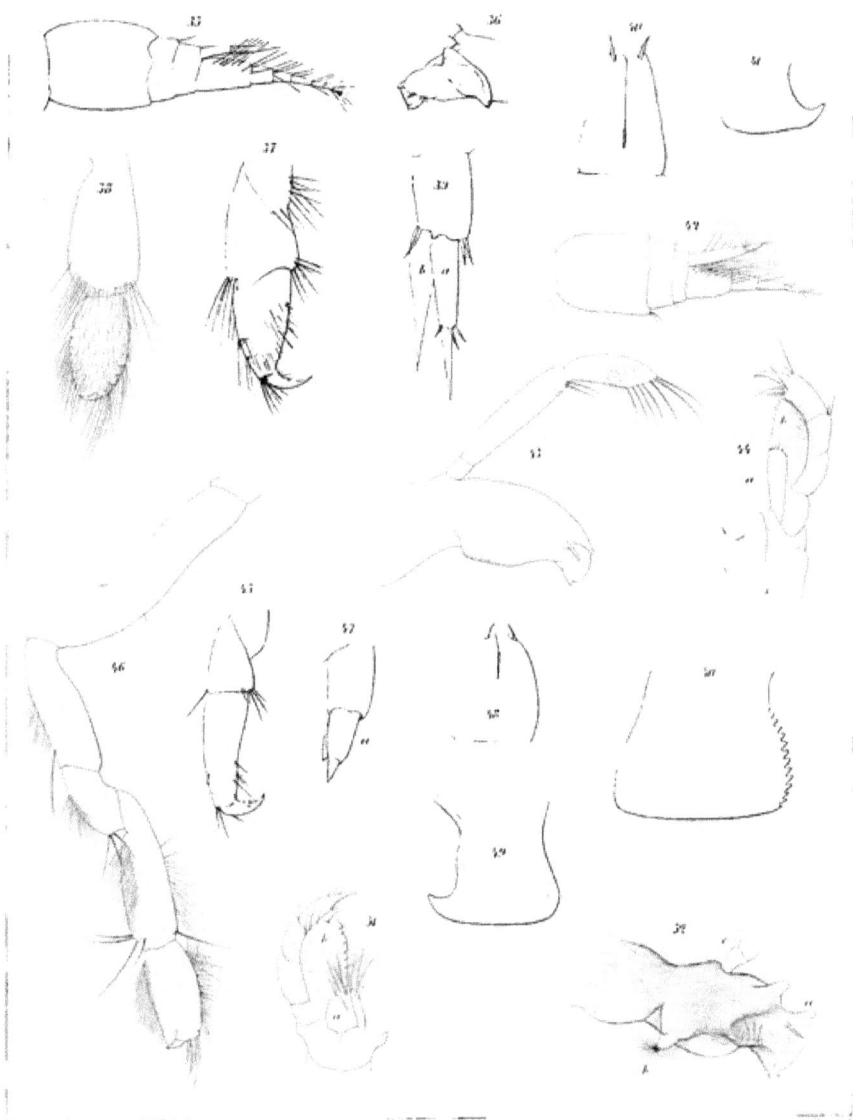

Fig 35-41 Anonyx pumilus Fig 42-49 Anonyx brachycercus.
Fig 50 Anonyx serratus. Fig 51 Anonyx tumidus.
Fig 52 Anonyx ampulla.

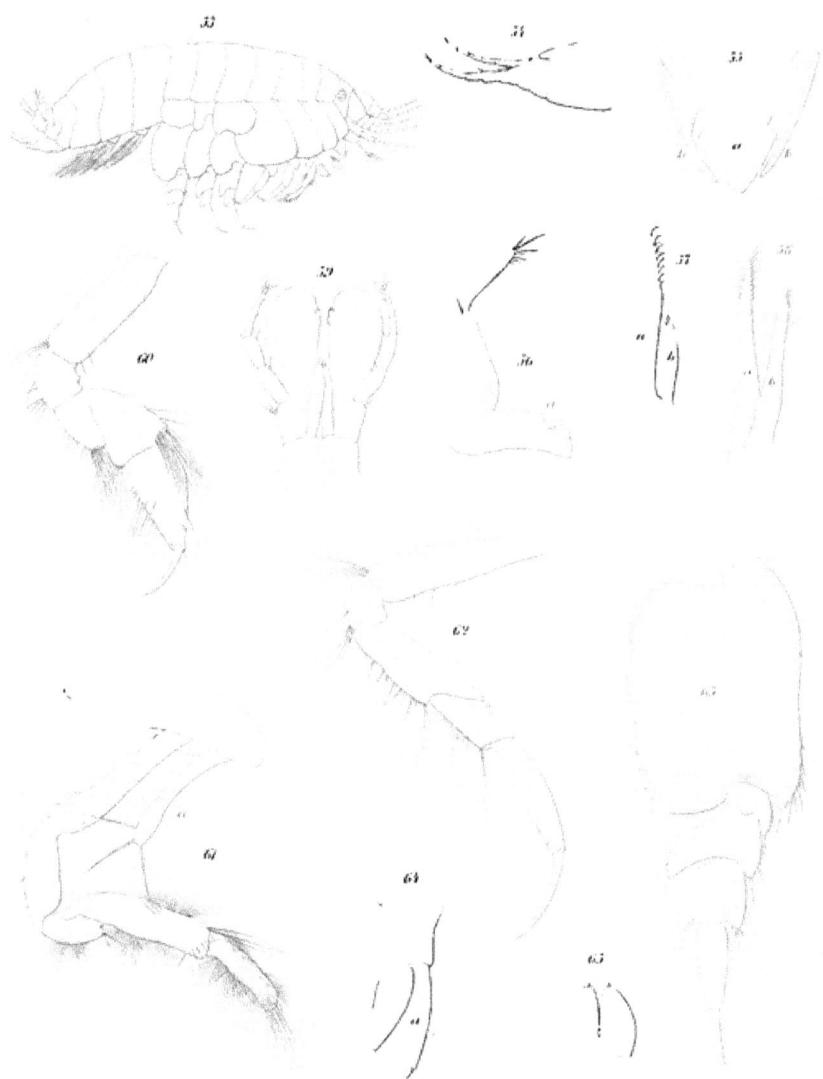